A
COMPILATION
OF LIFE

THIS IS MY MOMENT

This is My Moment: A Compilation of Life
Copyright © 2011 by Patrick Mitchell. All rights reserved.

MINDSTIR MEDIA

Published by MindStir Media, LLC
45 Lafayette Rd | Suite 181| North Hampton, NH 03862 | USA
1.800.767.0531 | www.mindstirmedia.com
Printed in the United States of America.

ISBN: [978-1-961532-13-7]

CONTENTS

BIPOLAR

From the earliest moments of my recollection, my mother's mental fortitude has been a delicate balance, teetering on the edge of instability. Her temperament was curious, prone to sudden and drastic shifts from one day to the next. As the sands of time trickled down the hourglass of my life, I gradually came to comprehend the enigma that was her psyche. With each passing day, my knowledge of mental health burgeoned, shedding light on the intricacies of her condition.

It was a gradual realization that dawned upon me like a slow-burning ember. My mother, who had always been a pillar of strength, had self-medicated for years. Her untreated bipolar disorder had been the culprit, and I had been none the wiser. The tumultuous waves of emotion crashed upon her without warning or pattern, leaving her adrift in a sea of uncertainty. The ebb and flow of her feelings were as unpredictable as the tides, and she could never anticipate when the next surge would overtake her. In her darkest moments, she found refuge in the numbing embrace of alcohol and drugs, unaware that her vices only intensified the affliction that plagued her.

My heart ached with worry for her, and I implored her to seek desperately needed assistance. Despite my earnest pleas, she remained resolute in her stubborn refusal. Her countenance betrayed her genuine emotions, yet she remained resolute in denying any distress. In the end, after much persuasion, she consented to seek the counsel of a medical professional. It was then that a diagnosis was made, revealing the presence of bipolar disorder.

As the treatment commenced, a gradual sense of emotional stability began to take hold within her. Her journey was fraught with peaks and valleys, yet the aid she was receiving made the lows more bearable and the highs all the more exhilarating.

The poignant tale of my mother's journey underscores the importance of engaging in open dialogue surrounding mental health and seeking assistance when one's emotional state is less than optimal.

From the depths of my memory, I can recall the earliest moments of my existence. A time when I was but a mere child, small and innocent yet filled with wonder and curiosity. The very recollection of being in her presence at home sent shivers down my spine, evoking a profound sense of dread and vulnerability. An uneasy feeling gnawed at my insides, a primal instinct warning me of impending danger. Yet, try as I might, I couldn't grasp what was amiss. My mother's perpetual tension was palpable, the air thick with her worries. Despite my best efforts to provide her with reassurance and comfort, my attempts were in vain as they failed to alleviate her distress.

As the years trickled by, the undeniable truth revealed a debilitating mental affliction plagued my mother. Her demeanor was one of emotional detachment, withdrawal, and a tendency towards fits of fury and impatience. My heart ached with the desire to aid her, yet I found myself at a loss for words or actions.

On a fateful day, a resolute decision was made - no longer would I wait for a savior to mend the broken pieces of my life. It was time to take matters into my own hands and become the architect of my destiny. My inquisitive nature led me to explore the realm of mental health care within my community, and to my delight, I stumbled upon a counseling service. As the sun rose that fateful morning, I knew my beloved mother needed medical attention. With a heavy heart, I scheduled an appointment with the finest physician in town. Though it was not an easy task, I mustered the courage to urge her to seek the care she desperately needed. The mere possibility of her recovery sent my gut into a tumultuous churn, yet I persisted in reminding myself of that notion.

The initial forays proved to be a formidable challenge to surmount. My dear mother, a woman of great fortitude, was relentless in her decision to keep her emotions locked away and shunned any notion of seeking assistance. As time passed, a subtle but undeniable transformation took hold of her countenance. As time passed, she became increasingly vulnerable and open to confiding in those around her, bravely sharing the depths of her inner turmoil.

The progression of my mother's therapy has been a tumultuous journey, fraught with the most challenging moments one can imagine. The space between her extreme highs and lows has been a treacherous tightrope walk, testing her resilience and fortitude at every turn. The journey may prove arduous for those seeking equilibrium amidst the tumultuous waves of euphoria and despair. One must constantly remember that the emotions experienced are commonplace and that one is not alone in traversing this tumultuous terrain.

To discover a wholesome approach to managing the peaks and valleys of existence, one must first acknowledge and embrace their innate and inescapable presence in our human experience. Delving deep into the recesses of one's emotions is an imperative pursuit, whether an introspective or extrospective endeavor. Acknowledging that life is replete with comparable fluctuations is paramount to this quest.

With bated breath, I eagerly anticipate the next crucial step in my journey toward inner peace and fulfillment. Without hesitation, they make the decision to carve out precious moments in their busy schedule for the sacred practice of self-care, for it is only through this intentional and deliberate act of self-love that they can truly thrive and flourish in all aspects of their life. By adhering to a consistent exercise regimen, obtaining ample rest, and consuming a wholesome and well-rounded diet, you can optimize your physical and mental well-being and experience a heightened sense of vitality. Discovering meaningful pursuits, such as cherishing moments with cherished ones, cultivating a passion, or indulging in soul-stirring melodies, can also serve as a balm for the spirit.

Navigating through the tumultuous waves of life's highs and lows requires a particular set of skills. Such skills are indispensable in the pursuit of a fulfilling existence. The mind and body can reap the rewards of tranquility and inner peace through relaxation techniques such as deep breathing and mindfulness. Moreover, confiding in a trusted confidant or a beloved family member can provide comfort and solace.

Maintaining resilience can be a formidable task in the face of circumstances that elicit intense emotional peaks and valleys. In this tumultuous world, it is of utmost importance to remain attuned to our emotions' ebbs and flows and be ever-prepared to nurture ourselves. Amidst the trials and tribulations of your present circumstances, I offer you a glimmer of hope. Allow me to impart some words of wisdom that may uplift your spirits and keep your head held high.

One must first come to terms with the undeniable truth that emotions are valid and that permitting oneself to experience them is acceptable and necessary. One must realize that emotions are fleeting and transient, a crucial aspect of the human experience. Instead of denying or suppressing your feelings, endeavor to comprehend and embrace them for what they are.

Next, devise a strategic blueprint for managing arduous sentiments and transcribe it onto paper. Deep breathing and meditation, historically linked to tranquility, may offer solace. Engaging in activities that bring you joy, such as indulging in your preferred sport or spending quality time with cherished companions, can be a salve for the soul. Behold, myriad exemplars doth present themselves, among which the ensuing is but a few.

The third crucial tenet in your journey toward success is maintaining a constant connection with your unwavering support system. One may find themselves seeking a seasoned expert's guidance and solace in their loved one's support. In moments of mental anguish, having a trusted confidant to turn to can make all the difference.

With unwavering determination, one must embark upon a physical activity journey and embrace a healthier eating and drinking lifestyle. Engaging in physical exercise is an excellent means of alleviating stress and other adverse emotions accumulated from daily life's rigors. To maintain a grounded state, one must minimize exposure to the ceaseless barrage of news, prioritize ample rest, and nourish their body with wholesome sustenance.

In the eighth chapter, we delve into the art of maintaining a positive perspective even in the face of life's inevitable peaks and valleys.

Maintaining a sense of composure in the throes of intense emotional turbulence can prove to be an arduous task. Maintaining an optimistic perspective can prove to be a formidable task when the erratic nature of our psyche perpetually oscillates. Notwithstanding the challenging obstacles, there exist methods to maintain an optimistic perspective.

As one embarks on the journey toward self-discovery, it is imperative to acknowledge the undeniable truth of one's vulnerability in the present situation. We can only begin to unravel the mysteries of our existence and unlock the hidden potential within by accepting this fundamental reality. Acknowledge and permit yourself to experience the emotions that are coursing through you. By undertaking this action, you may discover solace from the weighty emotional load that currently besets you.

Secondly, you must allocate a portion of your schedule for unwinding and revitalization. Indulge in a moment of respite and engage in an activity that you know will soothe your soul, such as taking a stroll, practicing yoga, or immersing yourself in the melodies of music. As you embark on this journey, you may feel less adrift and more firmly anchored in the present moment.

Above all else, one must make the preservation of their health and well-being their utmost priority. To preserve your well-being, adhering to a balanced regimen of wholesome sustenance, ample rest, and consistent physical activity is imperative. Do not chastise yourself excessively if adhering to a schedule is challenging; instead, focus on giving your utmost effort.

As you traverse the winding road of life, always remember to maintain a connection with those who have aided you along the way. These individuals have guided your journey, illuminating the path forward and providing support when the going got tough. Whether through a heartfelt message or a simple phone call, let them know their kindness has not gone unnoticed. Through the bonds we forge with others, we find the strength to overcome any obstacle that may come our way. Seek out a coterie of individuals who can lend their aid if you have yet to procure one. Engage in meaningful conversations with a confidant who holds your trust, whether a cherished family member or a dear friend. Consider seeking the guidance of a qualified professional or joining a support group to aid in your journey toward healing and growth. Merely reaching out to others can work wonders in lifting your spirits and improving your circumstances.

CO-PARENTING

The intricacies of co-parenting can be a daunting task for divorced parents as they strive to navigate the complexities of working together for the betterment of their children. When the bonds of love and devotion that once held a marriage or long-term relationship together are severed, the resulting turmoil can be a formidable challenge for all parties concerned. Amidst the less-than-ideal circumstances, one must remember the cruciality of co-parenting for the well-being of the innocent children entangled in the situation. Amidst the heart-wrenching realization that the one who has once been deemed the epitome of love and affection is now a former spouse, finding the silver lining may seem like an impossible task. However, it is imperative to do so, especially for the sake of your precious offspring.

In the arduous journey of co-parenting after a divorce, the initial and most crucial stride is to relinquish any lingering resentment towards your former partner and instead direct your unwavering attention towards the needs of your beloved offspring. The procedure hangs in the balance at this juncture, teetering on the edge of success or failure. The moment's weight is palpable, as every move made from this point forward will determine the outcome. Amidst the necessity of setting boundaries, it remains imperative to maintain a composed and courteous demeanor when deliberating matters that impact the little ones. In the sacred bond of parenthood, it is essential to acknowledge that your offspring require the presence and guidance of both progenitors. Thus, it is crucial to bear in mind that your former partner is, in fact, an integral figure in your children's lives as the other parent. Yet another essential factor to ponder.

Remember the immense worth of remaining open to discourse and embracing diversity. The art of co-parenting demands a delicate balance of adaptability and empathy.

Maintaining a level head and fostering a harmonious environment for your children can prove to be an arduous task in the throes of a tumultuous co-parenting relationship. When communication falters, and tensions mount, the emotional fortitude required to navigate these choppy waters can be daunting. At the outset, it is paramount to acknowledge the moment when your sentiments are obfuscating your discernment and disengage yourself emotionally from the episode, enabling you to assess it with clarity and reason. To succeed in this endeavor, one must cast aside all anguish and hatred and instead concentrate on the offspring's welfare.

In the intricate dance of co-parenting, one must always keep a level head when engaging with their counterpart.

Maintaining a sense of composure and collectedness is paramount to achieving a harmonious and productive co-parenting relationship. Pause momentarily, allow your mind to gather its bearings, and meticulously strategize your reply before engaging with your co-parent. By implementing this technique, the tint of your emotions will be less likely to seep into your comments.

It is of utmost importance to remember that co-parenting should not be viewed as a contest. One mustn't subject their child to the cruel and unjust act of ridiculing the other parent in their presence. It is a disservice to the innocent and impressionable mind of the young one and a violation of their right to a peaceful and nurturing upbringing. Let us shift our attention towards a collaborative effort to create a haven of security and nourishment within the confines of our humble abode, where our little ones can flourish and grow.

One must always remember the profound importance of exhibiting empathy and comprehension while communicating with one's co-parent. As you navigate the tumultuous waters of co-parenting, it's crucial to remember that your child's other progenitor may also be grappling with feelings of anguish or disillusionment—endeavor to sustain an open and transparent channel of dialogue for the sake of your offspring's well-being.

In the intricate dance of co-parenting, one must never forget the importance of placing the desires and emotions of the children above one's own. Above all else, one must prioritize the well-being of their offspring, regardless of the personal ramifications that may ensue from any given choice. By making choices considering your children's emotional well-being, you demonstrate your unwavering devotion to their happiness and place their needs above yours. This act of selflessness strengthens your bond with them and instills in them a sense of security and love that will last a lifetime. Demonstrating such selflessness is a testament to your profound affection for them and your unwavering commitment to their well-being. Crafting a welcoming and nurturing home environment is paramount to fostering the growth and prosperity of your offspring. It is crucial in their journey toward a fulfilling and triumphant adulthood.

One must never forget that co-parenting is a delicate dance of prioritizing the children's welfare and fostering a harmonious relationship with their other parental figures. Co-parenting is a formidable challenge, yet the rewards are immeasurable. It would help if you exhibited empathy and reverence towards the other parent's beliefs and principles, regardless of your hatred. It is essential to understand that disagreements may arise, but handling them with grace and dignity is crucial. Empower your children by involving them in decision-making processes. Grant them the agency to shape their world and influence future outcomes.

To truly excel as a co-parent, one must possess the ability to prioritize their children's needs above their own and find common ground on crucial matters through the art of compromise. Placing the emotional well-being of your offspring above your own may prove to be a daunting task, yet it is an indispensable aspect of co-parenting. With the well-being of the children at the forefront, co-parenting can prove to be a formidable task. Balancing the needs of the little ones with your own can be a daunting challenge, but one that must be met with unwavering determination. It would greatly assist if you wholeheartedly endeavor in that particular direction. One must always bear in mind that the needs of one's offspring supersede one's own, even if achieving equilibrium between the two proves to be a daunting task. Within the realm of co-parenting, prioritizing your children's emotions is paramount. Here are a few pointers to assist you in this endeavor:

Above all else, it is imperative to maintain an unwavering focus on the needs of your beloved offspring. One must endeavor to make decisions that are in the best interest of their offspring, for the family unit is the most paramount entity in existence.

Cast aside your emotions towards the other parent and contemplate what course of action would be most advantageous for your offspring. Amidst the tumultuous nature of co-parenting, finding common ground with the other parent regarding the welfare of your offspring can be arduous. However, it is imperative to prioritize the child's requirements and refrain from allowing personal emotions to cloud your judgment.

With bated breath, one must embark upon the third step a crucial journey toward emotional intelligence. Engage your little ones in a heartfelt conversation, delving deep into their tender hearts' recesses and unraveling their emotions' intricate tapestry. Can we hope to foster a generation of empathetic and self-aware individuals? One cannot overstate the importance of devoting ample time to actively listen to one's offspring and empathetically place oneself in their position. It is essential to convey that their thoughts and emotions are valued and appreciated.

As the fourth tenet of your journey, you must accept that you shall be held accountable for your actions. This inescapable truth must be acknowledged and embraced to progress toward your ultimate destination. In the event of an error, it is imperative to promptly recognize and express remorse to those impacted. Demonstrating to your offspring that you possess the maturity to accept accountability and the humility to glean wisdom from your missteps shall undoubtedly leave an indelible impression upon them.

FINANCIAL DIFFICULTIES

Financial woes have become a ubiquitous and formidable obstacle in the current landscape. You can work hard your entire life, scrimping and saving and making do with what you have. Your savings can grow ever so slowly but grow nonetheless. You keep your money carefully hidden away, daydreaming of everything you can do – start a business, return to school, travel the world. Day in and day out, you are devoted to your cause, and your money keeps adding up. But, one day, you make a series of bad decisions, and your money is gone instantly, leaving you with nothing but regret.

One can navigate these challenging times with the proper mindset and adequate preparation. Amidst the tumultuous waves of economic uncertainty, one mustn't lose hope. To weather the storm, one must heed the following counsel:

In the face of financial adversity, the first step towards solvency is creating a comprehensive spending plan or budget. With this tool, you can meticulously track your expenditures and establish attainable objectives for your financial future. One must select a hierarchy of spending and exert every effort to remain within the confines of their financial plan.

In the wake of a financial crisis, the prudent and necessary course of action is to embark upon frugality and thrift. Saving money is the cornerstone of this journey, a vital step towards restoring fiscal health and securing a stable future. With each passing month, allocating a portion of your earnings toward the noble cause of saving or investing is imperative. This prudent practice ensures you are always equipped with a safety net to fall back on during trying times.

In these trying times, we must tighten our belts and cut expenses wherever possible. We must be vigilant in pursuing financial stability and make the tough decisions necessary to ensure our long-term success. Let us not shy away from the challenge before us but instead embrace it with a steadfast determination to emerge more robust and more resilient than ever before. The road ahead may be difficult, but we can weather any storm with discipline and focus and come out on top. So let us roll up our sleeves and get to work, for the future is ours to shape and mold as we see fit. Reducing expenditures is a proven strategy for extricating oneself from a fiscal predicament. To amass a fortune, one must exercise frugality by curtailing expenses such as dining out and subscribing to cable services.

Embark on a journey of discovery as we delve into the realm of alternative revenue sources. Uncover the secrets of generating income beyond the traditional methods and unlock the potential of your financial future. Join us as we navigate the uncharted waters of innovative revenue streams and chart a course toward economic prosperity. The possibilities are endless, and the rewards await those who dare to venture beyond the conventional. Are you ready to explore the unknown and seize the opportunities that await? The adventure begins now. One must expand their revenue streams. The strategy entails exploring alternative avenues such as securing supplementary employment, leveraging e-commerce platforms to dispose of excess possessions, or capitalizing on available living space by renting it out.

A keen awareness of the available options can be the key to navigating a difficult situation.

Many individuals will inevitably encounter daunting financial predicaments at some point in their lives. The harrowing effects, both emotional and physical, of this ordeal could ultimately erode the very fabric of one's existence. One cannot overstate the importance of recognizing the challenges that come with a meager income and the measures that can be taken to alleviate the negative impact of such a predicament.

The formidable barriers of apprehension and unease that can emerge from a precarious monetary predicament are not to be underestimated. People in need are often besieged by a sense of powerlessness, grappling with many emotions, such as anxiety and melancholy. The weight of financial hardship can be crushing, leaving one feeling lonely, hopeless, and burdened with a sense of shame and guilt for their inability to adequately provide for themselves and their loved ones. Insufficient funds to procure the necessities of life, such as sustenance, attire, and shelter, can exacerbate an individual's anxiety and apprehension to unprecedented levels.

The tumultuous waters of financial hardship often bring a treacherous companion: a lack of stability in one's finances. The plight of the less fortunate is dire, as they struggle to fulfill even the most basic financial responsibilities, such as paying rent and utilities. The dire consequences of such circumstances are not to be underestimated, as they may entail the loss of one's cherished abode to the unforgiving jaws of foreclosure or the unwelcome prospect of having to relocate. People in need among us often find themselves bereft of the resources necessary to prepare for unforeseen circumstances or secure their opportunities for tomorrow. This predicament can profoundly affect their capacity to break free from the shackles of impoverishment. Such unforeseen circumstances can wreak havoc on one's financial stability, leaving them vulnerable to monetary woes.

The daunting prospect of financial difficulties can be an arduous journey for anyone. The tumultuous emotions of loss, insecurity, and worry can inundate individuals, rendering them powerless and vulnerable to the whims of fate. One must always remember that the current financial predicament is a fleeting moment in the grand scheme. Fear not, for there are ways to fortify oneself and remain steadfast in adversity.

The initial stride towards a fulfilling life is to possess an optimistic perspective. In the face of adversity, succumbing to self-doubt and despair is all too easy. On the flip side, maintaining an upbeat demeanor could be the key to unlocking your unwavering determination and concentration. Remember that this is merely a fleeting obstacle, and concentrate on the aspects of the predicament within your grasp. Crafting a particular financial blueprint and setting attainable monetary objectives may prove instrumental in remedying this predicament.

With bated breath, some may contemplate their next move. The stakes were high, and the risks even more elevated. Creating a safety net, a cushion of protection against the unknown, was imperative. For without it, the consequences could be dire. With a determined spirit, some set forth to weave a web of security, a safety net to catch them should they fall. In the throes of financial hardship, one may feel isolated. However, it is imperative to maintain connections with those nearest and dearest to us. When the world's weight falls upon your shoulders, seek solace in embracing those nearest and dearest to your heart. And when the complexities of fiscal management confound your mind, seek the sage counsel of a seasoned professional. In times of adversity, the true strength of one's character is revealed. To weather the storm and emerge victorious, one must have a robust network of individuals who can provide aid and comfort. With their unwavering support, you will find the courage to face any challenge and experience a profound sense of security.

Ensuring preserving your physical and mental well-being should reign supreme among your daily priorities.

The insidious nature of stress and worry can wreak havoc on one's physical and psychological well-being, leaving a trail of harmful effects in their wake. It is of utmost importance to tend to oneself diligently and consistently.

Inevitably, the harsh reality of financial hardship will befall many individuals. Perhaps it resulted from unexpected events, such as a sudden job loss, a debilitating illness, or unforeseen financial burdens. In the face of adversity, the task of lifting oneself by the financial bootstraps can prove to be a daunting one. Yet, the power of a positive mindset cannot be underestimated in such trying times. Resilience, the capacity to rebound from adversity, is crucial for those endeavoring to extricate themselves from a dire financial predicament.

Cultivating resilience is vital, empowering individuals to maintain their composure and strive for excellence in the face of adversity. One may be consumed by a sense of despair and hopelessness in the depths of financial strife. Those endowed with resilience possess a remarkable ability to maintain a positive perspective and accomplish objectives with greater efficacy. The allure of a better financial future is a powerful force, driving individuals to push themselves beyond their limits and take daring risks. With newfound confidence, they embark on a journey toward prosperity fueled by the promise of a brighter tomorrow.

Amidst the turbulent waves of financial adversity, resilient souls can often weather the storm more easily. Amid a daunting financial predicament, it is crucial to remember that brighter days are on the horizon. Those who possess resilience can withstand the most trying of circumstances, refusing to succumb to the weight of adversity. Instead, they rise above the fray, channeling their energy towards effecting positive transformations in their lives. Not only does it aid in enhancing emotional regulation and goal-setting, but it also fosters a sense of rootedness in the present reality.

In the throes of financial hardship, a well-crafted plan is essential. Those who possess the fortitude to rebound from adversity are the ones most apt to triumph in the execution of their aspirations.

FIND AND KEEPING
A GOOD BALANCE

As the weight of responsibility settles upon one's shoulders in adulthood, achieving balance becomes increasingly arduous. The human experience is a delicate balance, a juggling act of sorts. We must deftly manage the myriad of responsibilities that come our way, from the demands of our careers and financial obligations to the intricacies of our relationships and maintaining a healthy diet. In this fast-paced world, it is imperative to prioritize the art of self-care. We must learn to recognize that seeking assistance when the need arises is perfectly acceptable. Embarking on a journey toward success requires setting realistic goals and breaking them down into smaller, more manageable chunks. This approach ensures that the path ahead is more enjoyable and increases the likelihood of achieving one's desired outcome. Turning to the familiar faces in your life, be it trusted confidants or seasoned experts, can be a wise course of action. By maintaining a meticulous sense of organization and relying on the power of lists to keep track of your daily efforts, you will discover a newfound sense of ease in maintaining order and conquering your daily chores. Amidst the tumultuous journey of life, one must never forget that the maturation process is not a mere sprint but rather a marathon. There will be days when the path ahead seems impossible, fraught with complexities that threaten to overwhelm even the most daring souls. Yet, in the face of such adversity, one must remain steadfast, for proper growth and self-discovery are born in these moments of trial. As you embark on this journey, you must treat yourself with kindness and compassion. Allow yourself the time and space to navigate the twists and turns ahead, and do not be discouraged by the obstacles that may arise. Remember, progress is made one step at a time, and with each step, you draw closer to the destination that awaits you. So be patient, be gentle, and trust in the power of your resilience.

As one traverses the journey from childhood to adulthood, the weight of responsibility increases manifold. No longer can one bask in the carefree days of youth, for the mantle of accountability rests heavily upon one's shoulders. You must seize control of your financial destiny, securing gainful employment and nurturing meaningful personal connections. Above all, you must prioritize your physical and emotional well-being, for it is only through a healthy mind and body that true success can be achieved. In the hustle and bustle of modern life, you are carving out time for the people and passions that genuinely can be arduous. Balancing many responsibilities can leave one feeling stretched thin, with little time to spare for even the most essential of pursuits - including self-care. One must never forget that the maturation process is a voyage rather than a mere endpoint, which is paramount. As you embark on your journey, be prepared to face triumph and defeat. Yet, it is within your power to glean invaluable lessons from these divergent paths and forge ahead with renewed vigor. The art of self-care and the quest for balance in life is paramount in enabling individuals to tackle life's opportunities and challenges with utmost efficacy and efficiency. In the grand scheme of life, the fruits of adulthood are reserved for those who toil tirelessly, harbor a profound passion for their aspirations, and are blessed with the occasional stroke of good fortune. It is then that life's journey becomes a fulfilling and pleasurable experience.

Engaging in self-care activities is of utmost importance. Ensuring that one gets sufficient rest, consumes nourishing meals, and maintains a consistent exercise regimen are all vital components of a healthy lifestyle. Cultivating a robust web of individuals who stand steadfastly in your corner can be invaluable. In times of need, seeking aid from those closest to you is paramount. The unwavering support of family and trusted companions can prove invaluable. In the throes of adversity, there is nothing more valuable than a support system of believers who offer unwavering encouragement and sage guidance. Ultimately, cultivating resilience lies in embracing a sunnier perspective on life and assuming accountability for one's choices. Self-care, self-awareness, and communal reinforcement foster the fortitude to confront life's obstacles.

The mantle of adulthood demands unwavering fortitude from within. Enhancing our capacity to endure storms, maintain composure amidst adversity, and confront challenges steadfastly. Moreover, it grants us a profound understanding of our innermost desires and strengths, empowering us to make quick decisions that lead to success. The resilience to bounce back from adversity enhances our ability to tackle challenges, fosters stronger interpersonal connections, and facilitates a more harmonious balance between our personal and professional lives. To forge a formidable character, one must nurture a constructive self-image. To achieve greatness, we must possess the courage to embrace risk, the resilience to bounce back from failure, and the wisdom to glean valuable lessons from our missteps. Resilience is a vital trait for adults, as it enables us to maintain unwavering focus and productivity while fortifying our relationships with others. In times of uncertainty and unforeseen circumstances, the ability to remain composed and level-headed is a prized virtue. Not only does it allow us to make sound decisions amidst the chaos, but it also enables us to find the silver lining in even the darkest situations. Indeed, a positive outlook can make all the difference in one's life. The art of resilience is a crucial component of the human experience, particularly in the formative years of one's life. The ability to flourish amid challenges is a remarkable trait that empowers us to unlock our utmost capabilities in every facet of existence.

The journey toward adulthood is tumultuous, fraught with challenges at every turn. In the face of life's many obstacles, the ability to swiftly recover from failures is an essential trait. Through this resilience, we can conquer the trials that come our way and emerge victorious. Strength, the hallmark of a true champion, is the ability to easily navigate uncharted waters, triumph over adversity, and persevere in the face of insurmountable challenges. It is the mark of a warrior who can adapt to any situation, rise from the ashes of defeat, and forge ahead with unwavering determination. The actual test of one's mettle lies in the ability to persevere through the most arduous circumstances. The unwavering mental fortitude propels us forward, even in the face of adversity. The art of resilience is a vital component of successful adulthood. The ability to rebound from life's challenges with grace and grit is a hallmark of those who flourish in adversity. Resilience, the ability to bounce back from adversity, demands steadfast optimism, unshakable faith in oneself, and a reliable support system of trusted allies. Possessing formidable problem-solving and communication skills augments an individual's likelihood of triumphantly traversing arduous predicaments. A profound understanding of one's emotions, strengths, and weaknesses is an indispensable tool that can be acquired through introspection. To cultivate a resilient mindset as an adult, one must exert tremendous effort, possess unwavering determination, and uphold an optimistic outlook. Those endowed with such remarkable abilities have the power to conquer their aspirations and lead a life of utmost fulfillment.

Resilience is a remarkable quality possessed by those who can weather the storms of life with grace and grit. It is the ability to withstand the crushing weight of stress and hardship, to rebound with remarkable speed from the most trying of circumstances, and to forge ahead with unyielding determination in the face of adversity. The journey toward personal growth and advancement is complete with the indispensable element of maturation. Before cultivating resilience, one must possess a robust comprehension of one's emotions and abilities and a sound sense of self-awareness. In this fast-paced world, mastering the art of recognizing and handling stress is essential. It is imperative to be equipped with the tools to navigate challenging circumstances easily. To succeed in this world, one must possess the rare gift of introspection - the ability to gaze deeply into one's soul and assess their strengths and weaknesses with unflinching honesty. But more is needed to stop there, for one must also possess the discerning eye to evaluate the skills and potential of others and the limitations that may hold them back. Only then can one navigate the treacherous waters of life with confidence and clarity and emerge victorious on the other side. An exploration of one's psyche and the understanding of others can inspire a newfound sense of optimism and self-assurance.

FINDING LOVE AGAIN

Amidst the heartbreak and turmoil of separation or divorce, one may wonder if love will ever grace their life again. But as the saying goes, time heals all wounds, and with time comes the possibility of a new beginning. The journey of rediscovering love after a failed relationship is not easy, but it is worth taking. It is a journey of self-discovery, learning from past mistakes, and opening oneself up to the possibility of a new and fulfilling love. So, take heart, dear reader, for love may be just around the corner, waiting to be discovered again.

Divorce, a word that strikes fear into the hearts of many, is a tumultuous and intricate affair, particularly for those in their third decade of life. Its emotional toll is immeasurable, leaving one feeling adrift in a sea of uncertainty and heartache. Though the prospect of re-entering the dating scene may seem daunting, you can take a handful of measures to alleviate the anxiety and streamline the process.

Allowing oneself ample time to mourn the dissolution of a union and sift through the complex web of emotions that ensue is paramount. Permit yourself to experience the depths of sorrow and acknowledge that this is integral to confronting arduous sentiments. Once the tumultuous waves of emotion have subsided, one must delve deep into the recesses of their mind and contemplate the lessons learned. Such introspection is vital to understanding how one's past experiences have shaped their present self. Reflect upon your priorities and values, and accept that establishing boundaries in certain relationships is an inherent aspect of life.

It is of utmost importance to be truthful about your present circumstances, not only with those around you but also with yourself. Fear not to express your intentions unabashedly to be taken seriously in your quest for a new relationship post-divorce. Bare your soul and reveal the unvarnished truth about your metamorphosis wrought by life's trials and tribulations.

Once you have achieved a sense of ease and confidence, it is time to embark upon the thrilling endeavor of approaching strangers. To embark upon a genuinely significant commitment, one must first understand their counterpart deeply. Begin with pursuits pique your interest, such as pastimes or convivial assemblies. With this newfound ability, you shall possess the power to accomplish such feats.

The art of divulging one's emotions can be a daunting task. Thus, it is imperative to exercise discretion regarding the particulars of one's life that are shared with others. As one embarks on this journey, one must contemplate the extent of one's comfort in divulging personal information.

Striking a balance between transparency and self-imposed limitations is critical. As a seasoned conversationalist, one knows to commence a dialogue with nice pleasantries, allowing for a preliminary assessment of the other party's receptiveness to further acquaintance before delving into more intimate subjects. Such is the art of social interaction.

Discovering the depths of another's character can be achieved through the art of conversation. Engage in a lively exchange of shared interests, inquire about their unique experiences, and offer personal anecdotes to forge a deeper connection. Venturing beyond the realm of superficial conversations can prove to be a transformative experience. Divulging one's innermost thoughts and emotions can unlock a world of understanding and connection. Revealing the true essence of oneself can catalyze forging an authentic bond with another individual, thereby fostering the potential for a profound and meaningful relationship to blossom.

One productive approach to acquainting oneself with another is to engage in shared activities that appeal to both parties. It is a sublime approach to unraveling the mysteries of one another without the discomfort of divulging too much too soon. Engaging in shared activities that bring joy is a splendid method to acquaint oneself with another's passions, principles, and character.

Following my divorce, I embarked on a journey of rediscovery and ventured into the dating world again. It didn't take long for me to realize the paramount significance of approaching a new relationship with a crystal-clear vision of what I sought. Forsooth, integrity, and honesty hold great importance in my heart. Thus, any individual with whom I shall entwine my fate must possess these virtues. I yearned for a confidant, a trusted ally who could honor my desire for solitude as I navigated the labyrinth of my emotions. Moreover, I require an individual who can uphold their emotional poise while exhibiting empathy towards me as I navigate the gamut of sentiments that inevitably ensue a divorce.

In despair, I yearn for a kindred spirit who will lend a compassionate ear to my woes and offer solace with unwavering empathy. A beacon of light to lift me from the doldrums of despair and instill a renewed sense of hope and joy. To navigate the labyrinthine complexities of my situation, my interlocutors must possess a deep understanding of my predicament, reveal a willingness to lend a sympathetic ear, and proffer sagacious guidance when I seek it. Only those with emotional and financial stability can earn my trust and provide me with the sense of security I crave.

Moreover, I yearn for a companion who possesses unwavering courage and an unyielding commitment to both myself and our bond. The individual must have the courage to be forthright and sincere in their aspirations for our shared destiny and demonstrate a willingness to effectively convey them to us through open and honest communication. One must remain receptive to discussing potential issues or conflicts, as open communication is critical to maintaining a healthy relationship.

With a heart full of hope, I yearn to discover a kindred spirit who offers unwavering love and support and shares my enthusiasm for nurturing a thriving partnership. After enduring the trials and tribulations of a long-term relationship, the bitter sting of its end can leave one hesitant to re-enter the dating scene. The prospect of putting oneself out there once more can be a daunting one, fraught with uncertainty and trepidation. Reacquainting oneself with a familiar routine and establishing a sense of ease in the presence of a prospective romantic interest can be complex. Conversely, embarking on a dating journey with a newfound sense of independence and a rejuvenated perspective can be a revitalizing and fulfilling escapade.

The question of whether to embark on the journey of dating post-divorce is one that only you can answer, dear reader. Like a precious gem, the answer lies deep within your soul's recesses. Should you find yourself prepared to take the next step, venturing back into the world of dating with a newfound sense of assurance and poise, there exists no harm in taking a chance and giving it a go. Embarking on a journey of rediscovery and romance after a tumultuous divorce may be the key to unlocking the shackles of heartache and discovering the closure you've been yearning for. An outstanding opportunity presents itself to meet a stranger and find that your fortune and joy can be mutually experienced with another soul.

It is an exceptional feat to exercise patience and allow oneself the time to heal emotionally before embarking on the quest for a new partner. If one is not yet prepared or still grappling with the aftermath of a divorce, it is advisable to hold off on pursuing companionship. Allow yourself the luxury of introspection and self-reflection, dear reader. Take a moment to cultivate your inner strength and fortitude before embarking on the difficult journey of courtship. Only when you are fully confident in your worth can you hope to attract a suitable partner.

INTIMIDATED

Within me lies a formidable strength, yet even I cannot deny the tinge of fear that courses through my veins.

Despite my awareness of my strength, it remains a formidable challenge to confront those who endeavor to belittle me.

In moments of anxiety or terror, my mind becomes a tumultuous sea, rendering it nearly impossible to concentrate on anything beyond my ruminations. Though I can champion my cause and vocalize my needs, there are moments when I hesitate to do so, gripped by the fear of potential retaliation. Venturing beyond my comfort zone is daunting, yet veracity and honesty reign supreme, even if it stings. As I hone my vocal skills, speaking becomes increasingly effortless each day. My confidence soars to new heights as I master the power of my voice.

She repeated the mantra like a sacred incantation, a reminder to keep her head held high and her spirit unbroken. No one would be allowed to bring her down, for she was a force to be reckoned with.

The essence of my being is shaken to its core when I find myself at the receiving end of bullying. My self-esteem, that fragile yet vital aspect of my psyche, takes a severe beating, leaving me vulnerable and exposed. The arduous task of self-reminding is a formidable one, yet I persist, for I am aware that my intrinsic value is not tethered to the opinions of others. Come what may, I shall maintain a buoyant disposition and a steadfast gaze impervious to the naysayers. Misunderstood and underestimated, I am a gem waiting to be discovered. Others may cast their doubts and judgments, but little do they know of the true worth that lies within me. With unwavering determination, I lift my chin and stride forward with unshakable confidence toward attaining my aspirations.

My heart races and my palms become slick with sweat whenever confronted with a situation that instills fear. The mere thought of someone attempting to intimidate me sends shivers down my spine and sets my nerves on edge.

Anxiety engulfs me whenever I find myself in a potentially intimidating scenario. The atmosphere was uncomfortable, and maintaining composure under such oppressive heat was no small feat. My pulse quickens, my palms grow damp, and concentration becomes a formidable challenge. My heart races as I scan the room for an escape route, my instincts screaming that danger is near. Oh, how I longed for the courage to assert myself, to rise and defend my honor. Alas, I am now vulnerable and powerless, yearning for the strength to take a stand.

With unwavering determination, I have embarked on a journey to fortify my self-assurance and shed the shackles of fear that have long held me captive.

Each day, I feel a newfound confidence surging through my veins. No longer am I content to remain silent and passive, for I have discovered the power of my voice. It is a heady sensation, this realization that I can stand up for myself and express my deepest thoughts and beliefs. And as I continue to grow and evolve, I know this newfound strength will serve me well in all aspects of my life. With each passing day, I am relentlessly pursuing a heightened sense of self-assurance that encourages me to articulate my views and opinions fearlessly. With great care and consideration, I shall meticulously select every word that escapes my lips. With each passing day, I find myself growing more adept at contemplation. No longer do I rush headlong into the fray, heedless of the potential ramifications? Nay, I now take a moment to pause and reflect upon the possible outcomes of my actions before proceeding. Such is the mark of a wise and seasoned individual who has learned the value of prudence and forethought. I have intimately understood my unique strengths and weaknesses through the arduous self-discovery process. This personal development journey has been challenging and rewarding, as I have learned to harness my innate talents while acknowledging and addressing areas needing improvement. Each day, my unwavering belief in my potential and capabilities grows stronger.

In the face of threats, I have acquired the art of composure.

The indelible truth that I am the master of my fate and possess the power to defend my convictions, no matter how arduous the task, is paramount. With each passing day, my capacity to articulate my thoughts with clarity and poise is rising. The weight of pressure that once threatened to crush me is becoming a mere trifle as I continue to hone my skills and strengthen my resolve. Standing up for one's beliefs is a noble pursuit, a testament to the strength of character and conviction that lies within. With a heart full of courage and a mind brimming with introspection, I stand poised to face any challenge that fate may hurl my way.

Through my experiences, I have come to realize that there is nothing and no one that can instill fear or intimidation within me. With unwavering faith in oneself, the courage to take risks is born. Such is the journey I find myself on - self-discovery and personal growth. As the dawn of a new year approached, I resolved to embark on a journey of self-discovery and enlightenment. With a genuine desire to expand my horizons and embrace the unfamiliar, I vowed to gain a deeper understanding of the world around me by exploring the perspectives of others. Forging ahead with unwavering determination, I eagerly anticipate transformative experiences. With each passing day, my confidence in my judgment swells like a mighty river, coursing through the landscape of my mind with an unyielding force. And with this unshakeable conviction comes a newfound sense of purpose, a burning desire to make a difference in this world that cannot be quenched. Yes, I am but one person, but I know that my power to effect change is immense, and I will not rest until I have done all I can to leave this world a better place than I found it.

With each passing moment, I am honing my courage to confront my deepest fears and disregard any looming dangers.

As the sun rises and sets, my confidence swells and propels me toward my destined path. Each step taken is a testament to my unwavering determination and unyielding spirit. The winds of change may blow, but I stand firm, relentless in my pursuit of greatness. To conquer my apprehension, I must first comprehend its origin. With each passing day, I become more adept at asserting my true self and embracing the full extent of my capabilities. With a steadfast determination, I have taken it upon myself to fortify my defenses by establishing firm boundaries and honing my assertiveness skills. With a relentless spirit and unwavering optimism, I have resolved to seize the reins of my life and forge ahead with unbridled determination.

I feel a newfound sense of bravery coursing through my veins each day. The once-daunting prospect of trying new things fills me with excitement and anticipation. Once towering and impossible, my fears now seem like obstacles waiting to be overcome. I am encouraged by the strength I have discovered within myself, and I am eager to see where this newfound courage will take me.

With each passing day, I am encouraged to take daring leaps and explore uncharted territories. The thrill of the unknown beckons me, and I am eager to answer its call.

I am learning to embrace the exhilaration of taking risks and venturing beyond my comfort zone. The world is my playground, and I am determined to make the most of every opportunity that comes my way. As I embark on my journey of self-discovery, I gradually accept the notion of being the outlier, the maverick who dares to chart a different course. It is a daunting prospect, to be sure, but one that I am learning to embrace with open arms. Ultimately, it is only by venturing beyond the confines of the convention that we can truly discover our unique path in life. With a pounding heart and a racing mind, I am summoning the courage to place my faith in the instincts that have guided me thus far. The weight of this decision is heavy, but I am determined to follow the path my intuition has laid out before me. With each passing day, my unwavering commitment to self-assertion has grown stronger. The ceaseless pursuit of honing this skill has led me to a place of unbridled confidence in standing up for myself. As I navigate the treacherous waters of uncertainty, I am steadfast in my commitment to authenticity. Each day presents a new challenge, but I am resolute in pursuing inner peace and self-discovery.

I shall not succumb to fear; no entity or circumstance shall daunt me. If there's one thing that ignites the fire within me, it's unwavering conviction. I'll stop at nothing to defend what I hold dear. With a heart full of courage and a mind unyielding to fear, I shall face any threat that may come my way with unwavering confidence. With a heart full of courage and a mind unburdened by fear, I shall venture forth into the unknown, daring to push beyond my limits and take calculated risks without a second thought for the consequences that may follow. With unbridled determination and unwavering focus, I shall channel every ounce of my being toward unlocking my full potential and realizing my loftiest aspirations. Nothing shall deter me from this noble pursuit, for I am committed to giving it my all. Though my presence may be subtle, it shall be felt nonetheless. With unyielding conviction, I am compelled to be the first to raise my voice and take a bold stance whenever my beliefs are at stake.

The realization dawns upon me that despite their palpable presence, conquering my deepest fears is within reach.

With each passing day, I become more adept at assessing my strengths and identifying the myriad ways I can harness them for the greater good. With each passing moment, my faith in my capacity to confront the enigmatic future is burgeoning. As I delve deeper into the recesses of my being, I am amazed to uncover a wellspring of grit and perseverance I had previously underestimated. With each passing day, my resolve to take bold risks and navigate through the twists and turns of life's journey grows stronger. I am determined to stay the course and make the necessary adjustments to achieve my goals, no matter the obstacles that may come my way. Once plagued by self-doubt, I now heed the call of my intuition and act upon its guidance. My confidence swells like a mighty river each day, and I embrace a newfound belief in my abilities.

LETTING DOWN BARRIERS

In the face of adversity, how do couples endure? The response to such an inquiry is complex, as it is subject to many factors that differ from one union to another. Specific teams may prefer to engage in a collective discourse and arrive at a decision as a unit. In contrast, others may require solitude to gather their musings and regain composure. In some instances, the intervention of an unbiased third party may prove necessary to facilitate a mutually agreeable resolution. For specific pairs, seeking counsel or taking a hiatus from their union can be the panacea for their woes. Ultimately, the course of action taken hinges upon the intricate dynamics of the couple's interplay and the unique requirements of each individual involved. In the throes of discord, engaging in dialogue, exercising patience, and remaining receptive to compromise to attain a harmonious resolution is imperative. In romantic relationships, one must always remember the importance of mutual respect and collaborative effort toward a shared objective.

The query at hand presents a formidable challenge, for the resolution is contingent upon each case's unique particulars. The prudent course of action would be to carefully assess and attentively heed the sentiments and perspectives of one's significant other before embarking on a meaningful journey in life. Should the matter at hand prove to be of little consequence and not demand an excessive amount of your precious time, then feel free to proceed as you see fit, provided that your actions do not pose a threat to the well-being of others. Success lies in fostering open communication and collaborating harmoniously to unearth a solution that resonates with all parties involved. The foundation of a flourishing relationship lies in the pillars of respect and trust, which are inextricably linked to the capacity for candid communication regarding individual inclinations. The crux of maintaining a harmonious relationship is discovering the optimal solution that satisfies both individuals and making appropriate concessions.

With a heart heavy with realization, I understand that my unwavering sense of independence has become a formidable obstacle in my quest for genuine human connection. Though I have long cherished my self-reliance, I now see that it has hindered my ability to forge deep and lasting bonds with my fellow beings. I am a fiercely independent problem solver, determined to tackle any challenge that comes my way with unwavering resolve. Even when the going gets tough, I refuse to back down or seek assistance from others, preferring to rely on my ingenuity and resourcefulness to see me through. The notion of depending on others, even for the most trivial tasks, does not sit well with me. My reluctance has taken a toll on my relationships, for I have not always been forthcoming in expressing gratitude for my extended support. In the throes of life's unpredictable twists and turns, I have realized that I must embark on a journey of vulnerability and faith in those around me. It is imperative that I shed the shackles of shame and guilt and embrace the art of receiving assistance from others. To maintain the vitality of my relationships, I must surrender a portion of my independence and embrace the prospect of relying on those in my midst.

Surrendering my independence is no small feat; I have always been a pillar of strength and resilience. For a considerable time, I have resisted depending on another, despite being aware of the benefits it may bring. The mere notion that the individual upon whom I have grown dependent may fail to earn my confidence and depart from my life is a genuinely harrowing prospect. The sting of past wounds still lingers within me, and the mere thought of experiencing such pain anew sends shivers down my spine. The notion of relying on anyone other than myself is a daunting prospect, despite my gratitude for the assistance of a companion. Independence has been my constant companion, a loyal ally that has never failed me. From a young age, I learned to rely on myself and to be self-sufficient. It was a necessity, a survival instinct that I honed over the years. Looking out for myself became second nature, a reflex I never questioned. And yet, even as I navigated life's twists and turns alone, I couldn't help but wonder what it would be like to have someone by my side. The notion of utter powerlessness and dependence on another individual is a concept that eludes my grasp. Placing trust in another individual without relinquishing one's autonomy continues to elude me, yet I am gradually coming to terms with it. As I traverse the winding path of self-discovery, I grapple with the delicate balance between self-reliance and interdependence. The enigmatic dance of learning to lean on oneself while simultaneously seeking the aid of others is a formidable challenge that I am determined to master. The journey toward mastery is an unending one.

The significance of my contributions extends far beyond the confines of my existence. The individuals with whom you forge a connection possess the ability to imbue you with vitality and joy. To achieve triumph, one must acknowledge the necessity of assistance and graciously embrace it when proffered. To traverse the tumultuous journey of life alongside another soul, I must possess the courage to expose my innermost self and embrace vulnerability. For a relationship to flourish, one must communicate candidly and unreservedly with their partner. The daunting prospect of committing an error or falling short in pursuing novelty cannot impede my progress. The art of trust, the grace of forgiveness, and the wisdom of empathy are all essential abilities that I must acquire. Embarking on this journey can be arduous, yet it remains an indispensable aspect of any relationship that yearns to delve into the depths of intimacy. Only through unwavering commitment and tireless effort can I hope to achieve the success that I so desperately crave.

With a heart full of determination and a mind brimming with anticipation, I eagerly embrace the challenge in this uncharted entrepreneurship territory. The thrill of the unknown beckons me forward, and I am eager to discover what fate has in store for me in this exciting new venture.

LOSING MY MOM

The untimely departure of my beloved mother during my formative years remains one of the most harrowing experiences of my life. In a world full of uncertainty and doubt, she was my unwavering beacon of hope. Her love knew no bounds, her positivity was infectious, and her strength was unyielding. She was the only constant in my life, the one I could always turn to for unwavering support. The loss of her was a gaping void in my existence, for she was my steadfast support and trusted confidante.

At the tender age of seven, fate dealt me a cruel hand when my beloved mother passed away without warning. This heart-wrenching tragedy has reverberated through every fiber of my being, leaving an indelible mark on my existence. From a tender age, I imbibed the virtue of self-reliance and resilience in the face of life's vicissitudes without the tender guidance of my mother. The path to success demanded that I acquire the skill of autonomous decision-making and embrace accountability for my choices.

Furthermore, I was compelled to navigate the treacherous waters of sorrow, fury, and bewilderment that inevitably ensue following the departure of a cherished individual. In the wake of her absence, I was forced to delve deep into the recesses of my mind, seeking innovative solutions to heal the shattered remnants of my heart. As I traversed the tumultuous terrain of my emotions, I found solace in the written word. The canvas and the melody also proved to be worthy diversions, offering a respite from the chaos within. And in the darkest moments, my unwavering faith provided a much-needed balm for my soul.

The memories of my dear mother and the invaluable principles she imparted to me shall forever be etched in my heart, a cherished possession I shall hold dear till the end of time. In the wake of her passing, I vow to derive fortitude from her legacy and grasp every opportunity to me.

My mother, a steadfast presence in my life, was my unwavering support and closest confidant. She was my unwavering confidant in moments of despair, a beacon of solace and hope. Her attentive ear and uplifting words were a balm to my troubled soul, a salve that soothed my aching heart. She stood by my side, a constant presence in my life, always ready to listen whenever I needed to unburden my soul. Her perseverance and unconditional love lessons will forever be etched in my heart, a constant reminder of her profound impact on my life. I am forever indebted to her, for she showed me the true meaning of strength and compassion. Lost and adrift, I am but a mere vessel without her. Her absence has left a void that cannot be filled, a yearning that cannot be quenched. The world seems bleak and desolate without her light to guide me.

The passing of my dear mother has left an impossible void in the very fabric of my existence. Finding a suitable substitute proved futile, for none could match her unparalleled essence. Her absence in my life is a perpetual wellspring of disappointment. The words of solace that escaped her lips and the tender embraces that enveloped me will forever be etched in my memory.

I endeavor to embrace the inevitable passing of my beloved, yet the task proves to be a formidable one. As the sun sets on yet another day, I am struck by the overwhelming realization of her absence. The weight of her absence bears on me like a heavy burden, a constant reminder of what once was and what could have been. Each passing moment is a painful reminder of the lost love, leaving me with nothing but a deep longing for her return. In the depths of solitude, when the world seems desolate and barren, my heart yearns for her comforting presence. Oh, how I long to hear her voice, feel her gentle touch, and bask in the warmth of her love once more. Alas, she is gone, and I am left to navigate this treacherous journey alone. The lingering presence of her essence persists, even in her physical absence.

With a heavy heart, I knew my dear mother would want me to remain composed and persevere through the trying times. And so, with every fiber of my being, I resolved to do just that. The enduring love of my cherished family and dear friends, coupled with the poignant recollections of my beloved mother, serves as the driving force that propels me forward. With a determined spirit, I embarked on a quest to transform my outlook on life. Armed with the power of positive thinking, I set out to cultivate a more optimistic and fulfilled existence.

At times, the weight of my loss feels insurmountable, crushing me with its unyielding force. Yet, I know this anguish is a necessary and organic facet of the journey toward restoration. No soul on this earth could ever fill the void left by my beloved mother, yet I am gradually adapting to a life without her.

The path ahead seemed impossible, an endless journey of heartbreak and despair. Yet, she persisted, her spirit unbroken despite the repeated blows to her heart, for she knew that the seed of her strength lay in the depths of her pain, a resilience that would carry her through even the darkest days. The initial stride towards a fulfilling life is to embrace self-compassion. One must accept the undeniable truth that these emotions are innate and justified within oneself. Realize you are engulfed in a tumultuous sea of emotions, threatening to capsize your very being. Embrace the melancholy that permeates your being, for it is a part of you that cannot be denied. Rather than futilely attempting to banish it, acknowledge its presence and allow it to exist alongside the other facets of your being. Only then can you come to terms with the complexities of your emotions and find peace within yourself. It would help if you allocated ample time to delve into your feelings and devise a strategy to manage the agony that plagues you. In these trying times, it is of utmost importance to seek solace in the comforting embrace of our fellow human beings. There is no denying the therapeutic benefits of confiding in a trusted confidant. Whether it be a dear friend or a beloved family member, expressing one's emotions can be a cathartic experience.

As a powerful technique for taming the turbulent tides of your emotions, consider taking a moment to unwind and cultivate a heightened sense of mindfulness. Engage in deep breathing, or allow your mind to meditate on the matter. Engaging in yoga and taking strolls are among the many beneficial activities one can partake in.

Engaging in activities that bring about a sense of relaxation and enjoyment is beneficial. One could find solace in myriad activities, be it indulging in a beloved pastime such as immersing oneself in a good book, engaging in a riveting game, savoring the melodies of music, or simply conversing with a cherished companion. It was merely idling away, accomplishing naught. Escaping from a distressing circumstance can serve as a much-needed respite.

At long last, you must seek the counsel of a specialist should you find yourself grappling with overwhelming emotional turmoil. The agony that courses through your veins is palpable, but fear not, for with the guidance of a skilled therapist or counselor, you can acquire the tools to master it—individuals, offering a secure haven to find solace and comfort.

The permissibility of persisting in lamenting the loss of your mother is not viable. One must grant oneself the gift of time and space to mourn, for it is a natural and healthful reaction to grief. Though your mother may no longer be present in your life, it is imperative to recognize that progressing forward is advantageous.

It is imperative to remember that the road to recovery from a loss is not swift. Though some days may shine brighter than others, it is a natural inclination to experience sorrow and mourn the loss of one's mother. The present-day seemed to hold a glimmer of hope, a reprieve from the tumultuous events of the past. Amidst the wild waves of sorrow, it is crucial to anchor oneself to the buoy of happiness, even if it is fleeting.

Pause momentarily and reflect upon the woman who brought you into this world. Consider the depth of her love and her sacrifices for you. Let her image fill your mind and evoke the emotions that come with it. For a brief moment, allow yourself to be consumed by her profound impact on your life. Recalling her essence could be as effortless as regaling anecdotes of her, perusing snapshots of her, or indulging in the melodies that stirred her soul. As the weight of your sorrow threatens to pull you under, consider revisiting the cherished moments you shared with your beloved. Allow yourself to bask in the warmth of those happy recollections and revel in the joy they once brought you.

There exists no shame in seeking assistance when one finds oneself in need. In times of need, it is imperative to seek help from those with whom you have unwavering trust. Look no further than your inner circle of loved ones and confidants for the support and guidance you require.

Moreover, proficient mental health professionals can assist you in traversing the depths of your grief.

The loss of a mother is a wound that cuts deep, leaving a scar that may never fully heal. It is a natural inclination to believe that the pain will never subside and that the void left behind will forever remain. However, it is also essential to recognize that it is acceptable to continue living, to move forward with one's life, and to find solace in the memories of the past.

RELATIONSHIP

The arduous task of forging and upholding meaningful bonds with fellow human beings was daunting. As I gazed out into the vast expanse of the world, I couldn't help but feel like an outsider, a mere observer on the fringes of society. The weight of my solitude bore down on me, suffocating any hope of connection or understanding. It was as if the world had disregarded my existence, leaving me to navigate the treacherous terrain of life alone. The perpetual ambiguity that shrouded the dependability of those in my immediate circle instilled a sense of unease, rendering me apprehensive about forging intimate connections with them. The arduous task of being true to oneself was a constant struggle, for the pervasive feeling of treading on fragile eggshells loomed over me like a dark cloud. The constant need to validate myself to others proved to be an immense source of stress. The mere thought of basking in the company of others has always eluded me, for I am plagued by the constant fear of being scrutinized and judged for every thought, word, and deed that escapes my lips. The world felt like a distant and foreign place, and forging a profound connection with another human being seemed like an unattainable dream. With a heart full of trepidation, I mustered the courage to reach out to my fellow beings and sow the seeds of camaraderie rooted in honesty, dependability, and mutual respect. The weight of past experiences had left her guarded, unable to open herself up to others. The task of forging profound connections with fellow beings proved to be a daunting one for me. In my quest for emotional liberation, I sought the guidance of a counselor to impart to me the art of vulnerability and the ability to confide in others. However, the path toward self-discovery was riddled with obstacles and consumed much time. With each passing day, I have become increasingly transparent and reliable, a transformation that has paved the way for more profound and enduring connections. Though the journey ahead may be arduous, I am gradually becoming more adept at placing my faith in others and expressing myself with a newfound honesty that is truly remarkable.

Despite the presence of another human being, I was consumed by an overwhelming sense of solitude. A profound sense of isolation consumed me, as though the world had disregarded my plight. It was as if no one could fathom the depths of my struggle. In the depths of my soul, I yearned for a confidant, a kindred spirit with whom I could unburden my thoughts and emotions. My very being was consumed by an overwhelming sense of melancholy and despair, as though I were adrift in a vast, endless sea of isolation. In the depths of my pain, I yearned for a confidant with the rare gift of empathy and the ability to lend a listening ear without interjecting.

However, I found myself encircled by individuals who struggled to forge genuine connections with each other. Alone and helpless, I found myself without the confidence to turn to for solace or guidance. My heart yearned for a kindred spirit who could truly understand me. Yet, in the depths of my soul, I felt an overwhelming sense of isolation.

Since the dawn of my consciousness, a gnawing sense of incompleteness has plagued me, yet I remained oblivious to its source. Instantly, a profound yearning overtook me, a desire so elusive that it defied definition. I embarked on a journey of endless diversions, each more compelling than the last. Wealth, notoriety, a new career - I pursued them all with enthusiasm. Alas, all efforts were in vain.

As the sun's rays gently caressed my face, I was struck with a profound realization - a yearning to delve deeper into the depths of my being. The desire to unravel the mysteries of my soul consumed me, and I knew that this was the day I would embark on a journey of self-discovery. In the depths of my being, I embarked on a profound journey of self-discovery, seeking to unravel the intricate web of my thoughts, emotions, and values that had been weaving the fabric of my decisions. The task at hand proved to be a formidable challenge. It demanded copious amounts of introspection, deep contemplation, and meticulous analysis.

As I delved deeper into the innermost recesses of my being, I realized that my potential to make a difference in this world was far greater than I had ever imagined.

Through a lens of heightened objectivity, I could discern the defining traits that comprise my very being. With newfound liberation, I was unshackled from the constraints of societal expectations and empowered to make choices that aligned with my authentic desires. No longer bound by the opinions of others, I was free to chart my course and pursue a path that resonated with my deepest values.

In that moment of epiphany, a profound realization washed over me, illuminating the path to authentic happiness. Having relinquished all hope, I resigned myself to the elusive nature of that which I could not comprehend. A sense of assurance permeated my being as I assessed, and a profound satisfaction filled me as I embraced my true self. The adventure was etched into my memory, an indelible mark that time could never erase. Its profound impact left an enduring impression that I will always hold dear.

Trepidation coursed through my veins as I contemplated exposing myself to potential harm again. Nevertheless, I summoned the courage to take the plunge. Haunted by past wounds, I found myself reluctant to tell my heart about the possibility of further pain. However, I was acutely aware that discovering genuine love began with cultivating a deep sense of self-love. With a determined mindset, I fixated on my numerous commendable qualities - magnanimous spirit, creative intellect, and razor-sharp humor. It was a constant battle within myself, a struggle to convince my mind and heart that I was worthy of love. Day after day, I repeated the words to myself as if they were a mantra that could somehow penetrate the depths of my soul. And slowly, ever so slowly, the belief began to take root within me. I came to understand that I deserved love and was worthy of it in every way. It was a hard-won victory that I would cherish for the rest of my days. With a deep breath, I stepped out of my familiar bubble and into the unknown. The world was vast and full of possibilities, and I was determined to explore every inch of it. I sought new experiences, eager to expand my horizons and broaden my perspective. Meeting new people was both exhilarating and nerve-wracking, but I pushed past my fears and embraced the thrill of the unknown. With each step I took, I felt myself growing more robust and confident, ready to take on whatever challenges lay ahead.

Furthermore, I relinquished the habit of comparing my growth with that of others and instead honed my attention on becoming the most exceptional rendition of myself. With every triumph, my enthusiasm for self-discovery intensified, and my faith in my capabilities grew stronger. After a long and arduous journey, I finally arrived where I was willing to open my heart to the possibility of love. The trials and tribulations of my past had left me guarded and hesitant, but now, I stood at the precipice of a new beginning. With a newfound sense of courage and vulnerability, I was prepared to embrace the unknown and be enveloped in the warm embrace of love. With a heart full of hope and a mind brimming with determination, I embarked on a quest to discover a soulmate who could genuinely comprehend and embrace the essence of my being. It was a love that had eluded me for so long, a love I had yearned for with every fiber of my being. But it wasn't until I finally learned to love myself that it came into my life like a ray of sunshine breaking through the clouds on a stormy day. It was a love that was pure and true, a love that filled me up and made me feel whole. And as I basked in its warm glow, I knew I had finally found what I had been searching for.

The intricacies of love and relationships are both fulfilling and challenging. One must remember that sustaining such bonds requires a concerted endeavor and a profound comprehension of each other's perspectives. For a relationship to flourish, both parties must prioritize engaging in candid and transparent dialogue regarding their needs and desires. A deep and meaningful connection can be forged between partners through such open communication. The art of attentive listening, adeptness in negotiation, and the sagacity to acknowledge that one cannot always have their way are all indispensable traits. To establish a solid foundation, trust and respect must be the bedrock of any relationship. However, maintaining these vital connections requires diligent effort and unwavering commitment. To cultivate a meaningful bond, one must be willing to devote significant effort and invest copious amounts of time and energy. Patience and empathy are virtues that cannot be overstated in matters of the heart. It is crucial to remember that no romantic liaison can ever attain a state of flawlessness. One must always bear in mind the best interests of their significant other and remain receptive to surmounting any obstacles that may arise. With a concerted effort and heightened mindfulness, one can forge an unbreakable bond with another soul that shall endure the test of time and bring forth an abundance of joy and delight.

THE INITIAL STAGE

In the dawn of time, when the universe was a mere spark in the vast expanse of nothingness, there was a moment of pure potentiality. From this moment, all things were born, including the very essence of life itself. And so it was that the beginning of all beginnings came to be, a moment that would forever shape the course of existence.

In my early life stages, I grappled with a debilitating lack of confidence and a deeply fractured perception of my value. The relentless grip of self-doubt clung to me, hindering my ability to perform at my best. A pervasive sense of inadequacy plagued me as I was in a perpetual state of comparison to those around me, always falling short of the mark.

To overcome any obstacle, one must first hone their awareness of the language they employ in their mind. The power of carefully selecting each word and phrase in one's internal dialogue cannot be overstated. It is the key to unlocking the most effective approach to any challenge. In the face of a negative thought, one must act with swift determination and replace it with a positive, uplifting reflection. In these moments of adversity, we must summon our inner strength and fortitude and banish the darkness with the radiant light of positivity. Let us not succumb to the shadows of doubt and despair; instead, let us rise above them and embrace the limitless potential within us all.

To truly thrive in this world, one must acknowledge their weaknesses and embrace their strengths. It is a delicate balance, a dance between humility and confidence. One can reach their full potential only by recognizing and valuing both aspects of oneself. Within each of us lies a unique combination of strengths and opportunities for growth. Our strengths are the shining beacons of our abilities, illuminating the path to our most significant achievements. Meanwhile, our areas for improvement beckon us to embark on a journey of self-discovery and self-improvement, guiding us toward a brighter future. Fixate on those very things, and always remember to take pride in your aptitudes.

As the final thought, self-care involves carving out moments for indulging in activities that bring you pure joy and enveloping yourself with individuals who uplift your soul. By implementing this simple practice, you will experience a profound transformation in your self-perception and elevate your sense of self-worth.

With an unwavering determination, I shifted my gaze away from the world's distractions and honed in on the raw reality unfolding before me. No longer would I be swayed by the whims of others, for I had found a new purpose - to observe and understand the intricacies of life at its most fundamental level. With a few deep breaths, I would steel myself and remind my innermost being that I am worthy of meeting the gaze of others. With a measured gait, I strolled past them, gradually lifting my head to meet their gaze. My countenance remained stoic and calm, even as my eyes locked onto theirs with an unwavering intensity. I would constantly remind myself that every individual's intrinsic worth and significance, including myself, are equal and unparalleled.

If only I could turn back the hands of time and impart the invaluable lesson of acknowledging and cherishing the quirks that make each individual a distinct and irreplaceable entity upon my younger self. The significance of embracing every person's singular outlook cannot be overstated. In the grand scheme of things, it is a universal truth that we are all crafted with equal measure, and thus, there is no reason for one to harbor feelings of superiority or inferiority. Oh, how I yearn for the ability to impart wisdom upon my former self. If only I could travel back in time and bestow upon my younger self the knowledge that the opinions and beliefs of others are to be cherished, even when they diverge from my own. As I reflect upon my past, I cannot help but ponder what advice I would impart to my future self. I urge myself to cultivate greater empathy and acceptance toward others. To endeavor to view the world through their eyes and to appreciate their unique perspective. Only through such a lens can we truly understand and connect with our fellow human beings.

Moreover, I would remind myself to exude kindness and unwavering patience amid life's challenges. I would constantly reassure myself that perfection is an elusive concept and that each of us is simply navigating the tumultuous waters of existence uniquely. Oh, how I long for the power to alter the past! If only I could go back in time and impart the wisdom I have gained through the years upon my younger self. I would embrace empathy and forgiveness to extend a helping hand to those in need without hesitation. Alas, such is the nature of life - we can only move forward armed with the lessons of our past.

I would impart upon my younger self the wisdom that every individual possesses a unique offering to the world. Be it a wealth of knowledge, a plethora of talents, or simply the capacity to lend an empathetic ear, each person has something of value to contribute. Had I the power to alter the past, I would have imparted upon my younger self the wisdom to cherish those who graced my life and to express gratitude for their every deed.

As I gazed upon the bustling crowd, I couldn't help but be reminded that every individual harbored a unique tale within. It was imperative, I mused, that every one of them is treated with the utmost compassion and understanding, for who knew what struggles they had endured or what battles they were currently fighting. I remind myself that every individual harbors a unique tale within. I would impart the invaluable wisdom that every individual is entitled to a voice upon my younger self, and we must lend an ear to one another. If only I could impart one piece of knowledge upon my being, it would be to extend the same compassion and tenderness to myself as I do to others.

Amid adversity, I was lost and unsure how to navigate the treacherous terrain. However, through the crucible of experience, I discovered that the key to overcoming such obstacles lay in cultivating mental fortitude. Resilience is the hallmark of a true champion. It is the ability to rise above adversity and emerge more vital than ever before. To be genuinely resilient is to possess a rare and precious gift that allows you to bounce back quickly from setbacks and persist in the face of even the most daunting challenges. It is a quality that sets the great apart from the merely good and is essential for success in any endeavor. So if you want to be a true champion, cultivate your resilience and let it carry you to new heights of achievement and fulfillment. To lay oneself bare, concede one's errors, and remain receptive to growth and betterment in the wake of those missteps requires a certain level of self-assurance. At the core of resilience lies an unwavering belief in oneself and one's abilities, even in the face of the most daunting challenges. Resilience is the art of maintaining one's steadfast spirit and unyielding drive in adversity. At the heart of resilience lies the indispensable ability to scrutinize a challenge with a discerning eye and conjure a viable remedy. The art of perceiving the silver lining in every circumstance and leveraging it as a catalyst for more incredible triumph is paramount. Resilience demands a swift and efficient rebound from setbacks. The essence of true resilience lies in the unwavering determination to persevere through the most challenging circumstances. The courage to persevere in the face of insurmountable challenges defines true grit. The quality of resilience is a powerful tool that can propel you to great heights in life. It enables you to easily overcome obstacles and setbacks and forge ahead with unwavering determination toward your aspirations. With resilience as your ally, nothing can stand in the way of your success.

THERE IS NO GOING BACK

The die has been cast, and the path is set in stone. There can be no retreat, no surrender. The future looms, a vast and unknown expanse of possibility and peril. With each step we take, we move further into the unknown, leaving behind the safety and comfort of the familiar. But such is the way of the brave and the bold, those who dare to venture into the great unknown, driven by a fierce and unyielding spirit. And so, we press on, ever forward, towards whatever fate may await us.

Behold the tale of a young woman whose journey from poverty to the pinnacle of prosperity is nothing short of extraordinary. Her childhood was marked by the constant struggle to make ends meet, as her family lived paycheck to paycheck. Despite her best efforts, financial stability remained elusive, and she was forced to confront the harsh realities of life at a young age. Undeterred by the challenges ahead, she remained resolute in pursuing a meaningful existence, expending every ounce of her being to bring her aspirations to fruition.

With fierce independence and a willingness to take risks, she was able to craft cunning strategies to generate income and elevate her circumstances. She toiled away at many menial jobs, each paying a pittance for her tireless efforts. Day in and day out, she labored for long hours, her unwavering determination driving her forward. And when the meager wages failed to suffice, she resorted to taking out loans, her indomitable spirit refusing to be broken by the harsh realities of life. With every triumph, her confidence swelled, and she began to envision a brighter future for herself and her loved ones. She meticulously crafted plans to elevate their standard of living, fueled by an unyielding determination to achieve her goals.

With an unwavering gaze, the young lady confronted her deepest fears head-on and embarked on a journey of self-improvement. She made subtle alterations to her daily routine, each a small but significant step towards a brighter future. She began setting money aside, secured employment and returned to school immediately. She had forged profound connections with those nearest to her, who became indispensable allies on her journey.

With a tenacity that knew no bounds and an unwavering commitment to her aspirations, she achieved what she set out to do. She emerged triumphant from the depths of poverty, conquering the odds to achieve greatness in a realm that set her soul ablaze. Through unwavering determination and unrelenting diligence, she ascended to the pinnacle of her passion, a true testament to the power of the human spirit. With a newfound sense of bravery, she found the strength to speak out against injustice and extend a helping hand to those who had endured similar hardships.

The trajectory of her journey serves as a testament to the power of audacity and tenacity in carving out a path toward triumph. Amidst overwhelming uncertainty, she persevered and made humble yet significant strides toward her goals. Her tale is a shining example of the priceless worth of self-reliance and unyielding determination.

Swiftly rebounding from adversity has been the cornerstone of her triumph. Despite the obstacles that may arise, she was able to persevere and strive for progress. The young lady could weather even the most turbulent storms with unyielding resilience. Her grit has allowed her to persevere in the face of hardship, emerging from the depths of adversity with an unbreakable spirit. With a keen eye for self-reflection, she mastered the art of assessing triumphs and setbacks with impartiality, gleaning valuable insights from each experience. The experience has ignited within her a newfound appreciation for the silver lining in every situation and a deep-seated belief in her capabilities. Challenges are stepping stones toward personal evolution and progress in the young woman's eyes. Through this profound experience, she has gained a newfound comprehension of herself and the world around her. With a newfound confidence in her veins, she was prepared to confront any obstacle that dared to cross her path. Through the trials and tribulations of life, she learned to embrace change with open arms and seek out the hidden treasures it holds. The unwavering resilience has been her guiding light, illuminating the path toward growth and self-discovery. With each passing day, she became more adept at managing the tumultuous waves of stress that threatened to engulf her. Through sheer force of will and a steely determination, the young lady honed her skills and developed a resilience that allowed the young lady to weather any storm. The once overwhelming burden of stress has been transformed into a mere inconvenience, a minor obstacle that she can easily overcome. Her ability to manage stress has become a source of pride and a testament to the indomitable human spirit.

Furthermore, the young woman became increasingly inclined towards embracing uncertainty and venturing into uncharted territories. With each passing year, her inner strength has grown into a formidable force, a source of unwavering power for which she is endlessly grateful. Every day, she strives to fortify this strength, to sharpen it like a blade and hone it like a precious gem. She knows that with this strength, she can conquer any obstacle, overcome any challenge, and rise to any occasion. It is a gift that she cherishes above all else, a treasure that she will always protect and nurture.

THIS IS MY TIME

The present moment is mine to seize. There are unforgettable moments in life etched into our memories as times of unparalleled joy and fulfillment. These experiences make us feel genuinely unique, setting us apart from the rest of the world. These moments transcend time and space, offering a solace that cannot be quantified. Treating each moment as one's own is a paramount act of self-care and compassion toward others. It is a profound realization that every moment is a precious gift, and we must cherish it. As they journey through life, they shall unearth the most profound significance of their past encounters and hold dear the precious recollections of those moments in hindsight.

To truly grasp the present moment, one must first pause to reflect on the happenings around them. The key lies in honing one's attention to the present moment. As you stroll, take heed of the world around you. Allow your senses to come alive as you bask in the sweet melodies of the feathered creatures above, the gentle caress of the sun's rays upon your skin, and the delicate flavor of the atmosphere.

By entirely permitting oneself to relish the present moment, one can heighten their consciousness and admiration of its exquisite allure.

With bated breath, the moment of truth you had finally arrived. The time has come to express your heartfelt appreciation. With a deep breath, you summoned the courage to utter those words that would convey the depth of your gratitude. The purpose of our existence can be fulfilled through a myriad of means - be it the spoken word, the innermost musings of our mind, or the deeds we undertake. As you express gratitude for the present moment, you unlock a gateway to abundant pleasure and heightened awareness of the blessings surrounding you. One can achieve this by acknowledging the bountiful gifts of their life or simply surrendering to the blissful state of contentment and gratitude.

For me, the quest to discover joy amidst the most harrowing of circumstances has proven to be an arduous undertaking. I am compelled to pause and take a deep breath as I contemplate my present circumstances. Amidst the chaos of life's unpredictability, I am reminded of the power within me - the ability to steer the course of events by my response, for it is not the circumstances that define us but rather our actions in the face of adversity that truly shape our destiny. Amidst the tumultuous waves of worry that threaten to engulf me, I summon the strength to take a few deep breaths and shift my focus toward the opportunities hidden within trying circumstances.

In the journey of life, there are moments when we find ourselves at our most vulnerable. These are the moments when we are presented with the most significant opportunities for growth. In these moments, we must summon the courage to face our fears and embrace the unknown, for it is only through this self-discovery that we can truly unlock our full potential and become the best version of ourselves. As I pause to reflect on my life journey, I am compelled to ask myself the most arduous of questions: "What is the purpose of my current experience?" and "How can I harness this moment to elevate my being?" The depths of my discoveries often surpass the limits of my imagination.

One must always bear the utmost respect for oneself, a crucial tenet. The constant self-flagellation over my inability to alter the circumstances deleteriously affects my ability to concentrate on the measures within my power to enhance the situation. In the quest for self-improvement, I have discovered a few tried and true methods to succeed:

I seek counsel from those I admire, drawing inspiration from their wisdom and experience.

I take the time to recharge my mental and physical batteries, allowing myself the space to reflect and rejuvenate.

I establish attainable goals that serve as a roadmap to keep me on track toward my aspirations.

Amidst the most arduous circumstances lies a glimmer of hope, a fleeting moment waiting to be seized. With steadfast resolve and a clear mind, one can bide their time and wait for that moment to present itself. Being accountable for the truth is a weighty responsibility that I must remember. It is a burden I must bear for myself and those around me. The truth is a powerful force that can bring light to even the darkest situations. And so, I must be honest with myself and others, for only then can I be free.

The cornerstone of personal growth lies in establishing an unwavering connection with oneself. The tendency to become accustomed to the status quo and consent to how things are is a well-known phenomenon. However, when we confront the reality of our true selves, we are compelled to strive for growth and self-improvement, ultimately leading us to become the best versions of ourselves. To attain a level of authenticity in both our personal and interpersonal relationships, we must cultivate a robust sense of self-awareness. This entails embracing and owning our flaws and areas in need of growth.

The essence of our psychological and emotional well-being hinges on honesty. The arduous task of confronting one's truths can be daunting, for we often shy away from the discomfort accompanying such introspection. Should we choose to disregard reality, we risk facing formidable internal obstacles that impede our progress and hinder the attainment of our aspirations. One may also experience the overwhelming emotions of shame, guilt, and anxiety.

To truly uncover the depths of one's thoughts and emotions, engaging in a candid conversation with oneself is imperative. Honesty is the key to unlocking the hidden truths that lie within, and by speaking openly and sincerely to oneself, one can gain a deeper understanding of their innermost desires and fears. So, my dear reader, I implore you to take a moment to engage in a heartfelt dialogue with yourself, for it is only through this introspection that you can honestly know yourself. The art of self-talk involves delving deep within oneself, asking probing questions to unravel the intricacies of one's inner workings and habits. To embody responsibility is to assume complete ownership of one's actions and the resulting outcomes, whether favorable or unfavorable. The art of self-awareness encompasses our external actions and the internal dialogue that shapes our perception of ourselves and the world around us. To truly thrive, we must learn to recognize and avoid the insidious trap of destructive self-talk, replacing it with a more positive and empowering inner narrative.

To truly live an authentic existence, we must come to terms with our innermost sentiments, regardless of their perceived negativity. Delving into the depths of one's emotions and unraveling the intricate web of their origins is a crucial aspect of this journey. We hope to make sense of our innermost selves only by gaining a profound comprehension of what propels them. Embracing one's vulnerability is a crucial component of this journey.

With unwavering determination, I strive to become the epitome of excellence, for I yearn to be the very best version of myself. My sole motivation is to be the finest individual I can be for my own sake. The unmistakable signal of my commitment to self-care is the deliberate allocation of time for indulging in activities that bring me pleasure and tranquility. The art of mindful communication requires a vigilant awareness of one's words and thoughts and a steadfast commitment to honesty and kindness in all interactions with fellow beings. It signifies a willingness to confront oneself and venture into uncharted territories to pursue personal expansion and evolution.

To be the best version of myself, I must take ownership of my actions and ensure that my most deeply held values guide my life. To be truthful with oneself and others, and to steadfastly uphold one's convictions even in the face of adversity, is a hallmark of unwavering integrity. The mere suggestion that I am open to embracing novel experiences is a testament to my adventurous spirit. The display of my resilience in the face of adversity is a testament to my unwavering determination. Rather than succumbing to defeat, I view setbacks as invaluable chances to gain knowledge and enhance my abilities.

Nurturing both my physical and mental well-being is paramount in my quest to unlock my full potential as a human being. I relentlessly pursue a regimen of consistent physical activity, a nourishing and balanced diet, and ample restorative slumber. I augment my daily routine with meditation and heightened awareness, fully immersing myself in the present moment. With unwavering dedication, I strive to fortify the bonds that tie me to those who hold the most significance in my life, extending far beyond the confines of kinship.

Printed in the USA
CPSIA information can be obtained
at www.ICGtesting.com
LVHW091914101123
763623LV00005B/21